Nearaway Places

Driving to a Meal in Maine

by
Lois Stailing

NEARAWAY PLACES: *Driving to A Meal in Maine*
Copyright © 2018 Lois Stailing

ISBN: 978-1-63381-129-4

Design and production by:
Maine Authors Publishing
12 High Street
Thomaston, Maine 04861

Printed in the United States of America

On the Cover:
Spring Point Lighthouse and Breakwater in South Portland, Maine

Table of Contents

Introduction

This book started as a blog as a way for me to express my enjoyment and admiration for so many of the beautiful and unique places in Maine. As my partner and I would drive around Maine and explore new places, I often thought that other people would enjoy these places if they knew about them. So nearawayplaces.com was born.

We would often explore with friends and joked that we were "driving to a meal," so it seemed natural to add that feature to the description of the sites we visited. (Note that restaurants come and go, and even when they stay, some are seasonal. Keep that in mind on your adventure.)

Let me introduce you to some of Maine's most beautiful scenic and historical places. It's fun and exhilarating to discover a new place. And Maine has some gems! These places are near to you—or maybe a little farther away from you. Come along with me to discover some nearaway places.

The Constitution Tree

Sunny yellow forsythia on the right and sparkling blue water on the left bordered Route 209 as we traveled from Bath to Phippsburg on a recent Sunday. Our destination was the Constitution Tree, which has stood on a hilltop in front of the Phippsburg Congregational Church for over two hundred years. The English linden tree is approximately 75 feet high and is said to have been planted in 1774. In 1988 the tree was recognized by the National Arborist Association as the Constitution Tree. A plaque has been placed on the tree describing its significance to an earlier parishioner. The tree is surrounded by a wrought-iron fence with a unique tree motif.

As I stood looking up at the top of the tree, I thought of all the blizzards, downpours, and hurricane winds that this proud tree has withstood. Standing in the presence of something of this size and age has the effect of cutting one down to size—an experience that I think is good for the soul now and then.

The Constitution Tree shares the hilltop mound with a cemetery plot where Maine's first congressman from the district, Mark L. Hill, is buried.

The church, of classic New England style, dates from 1802; a stained-glass window in the front bears that date. There are several other old houses nearby that are also historical and very picturesque. Of particular note is the 1774 Inn.

The journey to the Constitution Tree traverses some beautiful scenery in both Bath and Phippsburg. To reach the tree, take Route 209 out of Bath, past the Hyde School. The road takes a sharp left at Winnegance (love that name!) with water on both sides and continues beside the Kennebec River inlets. In approximately five miles, turn left onto the Parker Head Road. The Phippsburg Historical Society is on the left, and soon you will see the 1774 Inn. The next left is Church Lane, which has a parking lot on the right. I would advise parking there and making the short walk up the hill to the Constitution Tree and the church. Be sure to look out on the Kennebec from the top of the hill; the views are well worth it.

Now it's time to eat. Head back along Route 209 and bear north, across the Sagadahoc River Bridge into Woolwich. Just a mile across the bridge is the Taste of Maine restaurant on the right. On Sundays in the spring and fall (but not during the summer months), they have an excellent buffet with choices to please everyone. Their extensive menu is always available, and seniors should check out their "Young at Heart" selections. We have enjoyed every meal we have had there over the years and recommend it highly.

In front of the restaurant is their "osprey cam" which streams live views to the restaurant's 42-inch TV. You can observe the ospreys nesting on their egg(s) and, after they have hatched, watch the parents coming back to feed the young birds.

Pownalborough Courthouse and Lady's Slippers

We chose an almost perfect day—the cloudless sky was a cerulean blue, and a light breeze wafted through the flower-scented air—to take a drive to the Pownalborough Courthouse in Dresden. The courthouse, the only pre-Revolutionary War courthouse left in Maine, is located off Route 128, on the banks of the Kennebec River.

A long gravel driveway leads to the classic New England-style structure. The setting is impressively regal as the white courthouse sits amid green lawns and nearby gardens, with the blue Kennebec River in the background. To the left of the courthouse are replicas of stocks and a whipping pole that figured prominently in punishment of that era—public embarrassment.

A short walk to the left on another gravel driveway is a cemetery where soldiers from the Revolutionary, 1812, and Civil Wars rest, their graves marked by American flags.

The Pownalborough Courthouse was built in 1761 from a design by Gershom Flagg, a Boston architect. The peaceful, pastoral setting today belies the bustle surrounding the courthouse in past centuries, as it also served as a tavern, a church, a post office, and an all-around gathering place for the young town of Dresden in Lincoln County.

The courthouse has an illustrious history, having been visited by John Adams, John Hancock, and Benedict Arnold. One particularly notable trial became the basis of *The Midwife's Tale*, by Laurel Thatcher Ulrich, based on the diary of local resident Martha Ballard.

The courthouse today is a museum of colonial life and has been very well preserved by the Lincoln County Historical Association. Unfortunately, we visited just before the courthouse opened for public tours during the summer season. The pictures I have seen and the descriptions I have read have piqued my interest, and I plan to return to tour the museum later this summer.

When my partner and I travel around the state, we often take side jaunts from our prescribed route. On our way to Dresden, we turned off on a gravel road that looked interesting. The road wound through forested areas that seemed to be perfect habitat for lady's slippers. We began scrutinizing the sides of the roadway and eventually spotted two areas of delicate pink lady's slippers, members of the orchid family. These flowers are becoming rare and are considered endangered. Spotting an animal, bird, or flower on a side jaunt makes that day extra special to us.

On this day, we opted for a cold treat and visited one of our favorite ice cream parlors, the Witch Spring Hill Ice Cream shop at 60 State Road, West Bath. This immaculately manicured stand has been at this location, serving renowned Round Top (from Damariscotta) ice cream for about five years. In addition, they offer hot dogs with a variety of toppings, pizza, and yummy ice cream cakes. There is outside seating and a play area for the kids. On a hot, humid summer day, there is nothing like their orange sherbet.

To get to the Pownalborough Courthouse, we took Route 1, turned onto Route 127 in Woolwich, and then turned left onto Route 128 and traveled 12 or 13 miles to the courthouse. The drive is extremely scenic, passing through an area of older homes in Day's Ferry. If you travel on this route, be sure to enjoy the territory you are passing through.

It's 10:00 p.m.; Do You Know
Where Your Cows Are?

This might seem like a silly question, but in colonial America, stray animals were a serious problem. Individual farms were close together, dictated by the need for security. Fences were rare because they used valuable time and resources to build. If crops were trampled by cows, sheep, or horses, it could mean near-starvation in the coming winter. It was a serious offense to let your animals wander at will and destroy your neighbor's crops.

To control this truancy, strict rules were promulgated, and stone enclosures called cattle pounds were built. Specifications were drawn up and were recorded in town minutes. The following quote from the town of Pownal records specifying the size and materials indicates how important the pound was to the town: "…to build said Pound thirty-six feet square in size. Voted

the wall of said Pound to be four feet thick at the bottom and eighteen inches at the top and six feet in height with a cap of timber nine inches square on the top of said wall with a good gate." The records also show that the town voted fifty dollars to build the pound and chose Thomas Cotton as its first pound-keeper.

Other towns that have pounds show similar specific instructions for their construction. They came in all shapes: square, oblong, round. Fines were established, and owners had to pay to retrieve their animals. The pound-keeper had to be a tough enforcer. Some of Pownal's fines in the year 1835 were: "For each horse, 25¢ for every 24 hours. For each cow, 13¢ for every 24 hours." Cold, hard cash; the pound-keeper was not a popular man!

One of the earliest pounds in Maine was the one in Harpswell, built in 1793. Two walls had to be reconstructed, and today the pound stands as a prime example of this forgotten part of our history.

The town of Turner had a pound-keeper as early as 1788 and an early pound in 1795. In 1816, the town authorized a new pound which was built at the intersection of the General Turner Road and the Kennebec Trail. This pound has been restored and can be seen today. It was added to the National Register of Historic Places in 2009.

An interesting sidelight of these "livestock lockups" was the practice of notching cattle's ears for identification. The town of Pownal called these "creature marks" and maintained a "Book of Creature Marks." All owners of cattle were required to mark their animals with the mark assigned to them by the pound-keeper. He could then identify the owners of the impounded animals and levy the appropriate fine.

Since I discovered the cattle pound in Pownal, I have been fascinated by them. I think this is because, compared to Europe, there are so few truly old structures in America. We have colonial houses dating from the seventeenth and eighteenth centuries, but cattle pounds are unique in structure and purpose. The concept originated in Europe and was brought to the New World by the early settlers. In 1821, the Maine Legislature mandated that each town erect a pound to control wandering animals.

For an interesting excursion to see something new (or something you may have seen before, but not realized its significance), take a drive to one of the pounds near you. There are about two dozen identifiable pounds left in Maine. Some of the pounds that can be visited are in Acton, Bethel, Orrington, Jefferson, Deer Isle, Waldoboro, Vienna, Porter, Pittsfield, and Lebanon. When you find one, take a few minutes to picture it in its heyday (this could be a pun!) when cattle were lowing, and the pound-keeper was

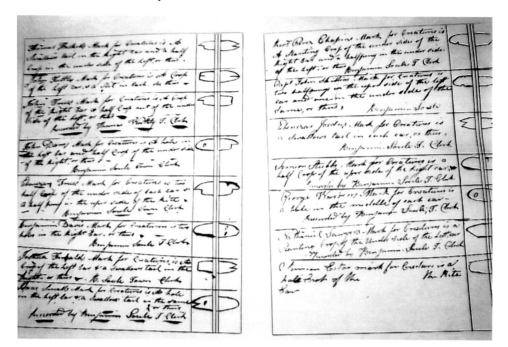

berating the scofflaw farmer while exacting the fine. Not very different from scofflaw misdemeanors of today.

As always, we ended our excursion with a meal. This time we chose Nezinscot Farm, an organic farm and café located at 284 Turner Center Road in Turner, about 10 or 15 minutes from the pound. The café serves brunch, lunch, and tea, and everything is made or grown right there on the farm. The farm raises cows, hogs, goats, sheep, and chickens and sells and serves the meat and poultry products. They make their own cheese and bake bread and tempting bakery items. Samples of cheese, sausage, jams and jellies, and baked goods are plentiful. You may come hungry, but there's no excuse to leave that way.

Beauty and the Shoreway

The views of Casco Bay from the Spring Point Shoreway are spectacular. As you look out onto the ocean, islands bask like jewels, and white sailboats float on the sparkling waters. In early summer, wild roses creep along the fence, and fruit trees wear their colorful blossoms. Put this all together on a day when the sky is blue, and you can see one of the most beautiful sights in the world. And it is right here in southern Maine.

The 1.6 mile walking path that constitutes the shoreway winds along the seacoast from Willard Beach, in South Portland across the Southern Maine Community College campus to Spring Point breakwater. The college and the shoreway are on land that has been home to several forts over the centuries. The last, Fort Preble, was deactivated after World War II. The part of the shoreway that approaches Spring Point crosses over an area of bunkers and fortifications and is the highest part of the trail. There are benches there

where visitors can sit and savor the spectacular view.

I like to sit on one of these benches and admire the panorama of Casco Bay and its islands. My thoughts usually wander to the horizon and beyond. For centuries, people have spent hours looking at horizons and wondering what lies out there. One of these benches is the perfect spot for beyond-the-horizon contemplation.

As you look down toward Spring Point from that height, you observe several stone fortifications surrounding a large grassy area. This is an ideal playground for the younger crowd. Portals through the stone walls are the perfect spots for youthful imaginations to pretend to be pirates, soldiers, or superheroes.

Along one part of the trail is the Shoreway Arboretum, where many species of trees and shrubs are planted. The arboretum, with its flowering shrubs and varied shades of green, lends another aspect of beauty to this spot. Meander down this path with an ocean breeze at your back and the scent of roses wafting through the air, and life is just about complete.

An added bonus of the shoreway are the views of two lighthouses that can be seen—renowned Portland Headlight to the right and Spring Point Lighthouse to the left. On certain weekends during the summer months, the Spring Point Lighthouse is open to the public. Spring Point Lighthouse was constructed in 1897 and was tended by a lighthouse keeper until it was automated in 1934. You can reach it by walking out on the causeway, built in 1951.

The oldest landmark in South Portland, the Old Settlers' Cemetery, also known as the Thrasher Cemetery, dates from 1658 and is located here along the shoreway. The oldest markers are just stones jutting out of the ground. Those jutting stones are stark reminders of how harsh life was in the early centuries of our nation.

And I must not neglect to mention that Willard Beach is just below the shoreway. If you want to spend a complete day here, you might want to include some beach time. Just remember to check the times of high and low tides.

Now, when it's time to eat, I am deviating from the usual course of selecting a nearby restaurant. Along the shoreway is a covered picnic shelter. It is well maintained, and you can sit there amid the greenery and admire beautiful Casco Bay. So bring sandwiches with you, take in the view, and appreciate how fortunate we are to have this marvelous place available for free.

To reach the shoreway, cross the Casco Bay Bridge from Portland to South Portland and bear left onto Broadway. Go to the end of Broadway and turn right onto Benjamin Pickett Street; go to the end and turn left onto Fort Road. The college parking lots are on the right just a little way up the slope and are available when college isn't in session. Or if you prefer, you can keep driving up the slight hill and then down to a smaller parking area near the Spring Point causeway.

NEARAWAY PLACES

If you continue to drive toward the causeway, you will pass a small white church on the left. It is called All Faiths Chapel and seats 40. This charming chapel is maintained by the college and can be rented for weddings.

Mile by Mile

Travel in colonial times was extremely uncomfortable and unpredictable. Many roads were little more than rut-filled dirt tracks that became impassable during rainy and snowy weather. Depending on road conditions, travelers could easily become lost, as they lacked the road maps and informational signs that we have today.

In the mid 1700s, British officials recognized the increasing need for a more reliable network of roads in the American colonies. They began planning and construction of a road from Boston to Machias called the King's Highway.

Meanwhile, in the colonies, Benjamin Franklin had been appointed joint postmaster general by the British government. As part of his duties, he conducted inspections of the roads that were used for delivering mail. Since one method of charging for postal service was by mileage, Franklin invented

an odometer to more accurately measure mileage. This device was used to delineate mileage on roads that were designated as post roads. In Maine, the King's Highway was used to deliver mail from Boston to Machias, and each mile was marked by Mr. Franklin's new odometer. Thus, the King's Highway morphed into the Post Road.

A marker, usually a stone, was erected at each mile and was chiseled with the number of miles from Boston. Town records indicate that these markers were placed in the early 1760s. Some of these stones, pre-dating our Revolutionary War, are still in existence today—over 250 years later.

These markers also served as beacons to assure travelers they were still on the correct road and to let them know how far they were from Boston, or from an inn.

I recently decided it would be fun to see how many of the existing markers we could find and so we made several sleuthing excursions.

On Old County Road (which runs off Captain Thomas Road) in Ogunquit, there is a marker on private property. It is marked with 69—meaning 69 miles to Boston.

In South Portland another marker is located on Westbrook Street, near the golf course. This marker is very close to a private driveway; it's marked with B 122 (122 miles to Boston on the Old King's Highway).

Note that each of these locations has a plaque saying the marker was erected in 1761 by order of Benjamin Franklin.

Markers for miles 135 and 136 are located in Cumberland. Number 135 is in front of the property known as Top Knot Farm on the Middle Road. Number 136 is located on Route 88 near the Town Landing Road.

The plaques in South Portland, Cumberland, and Yarmouth indicate that they were erected by Cumberland County.

In Yarmouth, we found 137 and 138. Number 137 is on Route 88 on the left side, heading north. If you view these markers close up, the mile number is clearly legible. They don't stand out as well in the size of the pictures here. Number 138 is on Pleasant Street, embedded in a wall in front of a house there.

My car's odometer registered 1.1 miles between 137 and 138. I think that extra tenth of a mile is acceptable, as today's Pleasant Street is curved, probably adding a little more distance between the two markers.

It is a fun afternoon excursion to travel to these markers and reflect that it would have taken many more hours, certainly more than one day, to make this journey in 1761 when these markers were erected.

Since these markers are located in several different towns, I am leaving it up to you to choose a restaurant or ice cream stand for your meal. It will add to your enjoyment to find a new restaurant to visit!

It's High Time

Now that the hectic holiday season is over, it's time for a jaunt to check out another interesting site in Maine. Over the years, I have had occasion to travel on Route 9 to Kennebunkport many times. I have always been intrigued by the large white farmhouse with the high clock tower on the Goose Rocks Road where it crosses Route 9 in Kennebunkport. This seemed like a good time to solve the mystery of why the clock and tower are there.

On one of the near-zero days that we have experienced recently, we braved the polar atmosphere and set out for Route 9. As I have gotten older, I've learned to appreciate the surrounding landscape in all seasons and at all temperatures. The temperature was frigid, but the sky was electric blue, and the fields were shimmering meadows of white satin, contributing to the mystique of winter.

This time, as we approached the intersection where the farmhouse is located, we turned right from Route 9 onto Goose Rocks Road. Facing the farmhouse head on, we could see a plaque on the barn which identifies the house as the Emmons Clock Farm. This farmhouse is a handsome white frame building of which the earliest part was built in 1773, with additions added during the next century. It has been kept in excellent condition. The attached barn supports a high tower with a very large clock.

With the name of the farmhouse, I was able to do some research and easily found the story of its clock.

In the 1890s the farmhouse was owned as a summer residence by the Emmons family of Massachusetts. Mr. Grosvenor "Gros" Emmons owned a factory in Lawrence, Massachusetts. He must have been well-liked as an employer, because records show that his employees contributed $250 and bought a clock from the Howard Clock Company for their boss. Mr. Emmons built a tower on his factory and had the clock installed there. However, the clock proved to be a source of disagreement, as the employees felt that it didn't keep accurate time. Mr. Emmons decided the way to end the dispute was to move the clock to his summer home in Kennebunkport.

The Howard Clock Company was hired to move the clock and prevailed on Mr. Emmons to spend $1000 to upgrade to a better clock! He did so and built the tower on the barn to display the new clock. Another interesting fact I discovered is that the farmstead was threatened by the fires of 1947. An adjacent building known as the servants' quarters was destroyed, but the Clock Farm itself was saved because a smaller fire was started to create a back draft that spared the farm.

Now I can cross another item off my "wish I knew" list, as I know the story of the clock in the high tower.

As usual, we also used this trip to visit a new restaurant in the area. We chose Run of the Mill Public House and Brewery in one of the old mill complexes in Saco. The interior of the restaurant has preserved the original hardwood floors and brick walls. There are many old artifacts, including mill pictures, which contribute to the historical ambience. There were four in our party, and we all enjoyed quite different meals. Organic produce is offered when possible, and the menu has a variety of choices. Run of the Mill is also a micro-brewery with a wide selection of brews. We are happy to add Run of the Mill to the menu of restaurants that we intend to visit again.

Run of the Mill Restaurant is located at 100 Main Street, Saco, not far from the Amtrak Downeaster train station.

There's More to Poland Spring than Water

The air on top of Ricker Hill, where the Poland Spring Resort is located, is as fresh as the water from the spring under the hill. We drove up there on a beautiful blue-sky day to tour the Poland Spring complex. If you haven't been there, it is well worth the trip; there is so much more to Poland Spring besides water.

The site of the once world-famous resort is the top of Ricker Hill off Route 26. On the way up the hill, there are two pillars announcing this as a "Stress Free Zone." As you drive through the expanse of green lawns and flower beds you find yourself relaxing; the sign is right.

As you arrive at the top of the hill, the Maine State Building is on the left and the All Souls Chapel on the right. The chapel, whose first service was in 1912, is a splendid little church surrounded by green lawns and a colorful garden. There are stained-glass windows and a charming interior made of

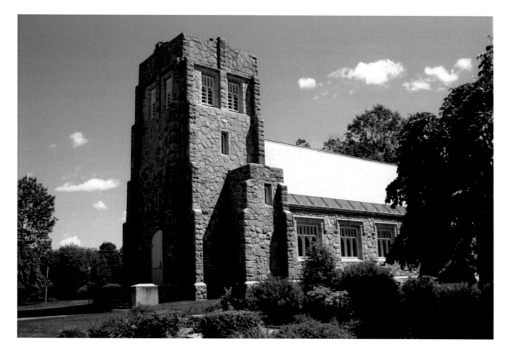

Maine granite, marble and wood, and it is available to all denominations. Over the decades, this chapel has been the site of countless weddings and christenings. One can easily see why—the site is simply gorgeous.

The quirky-looking Maine State Building, with its garrets, balconies, and conical tower-tops, is a true gem with a remarkable history. It was constructed for exhibition at the Columbian Exposition of 1893 in Chicago. The building is octagonal in shape and was made of Maine granite and wood by leading Maine craftsmen of that era. After the exposition, Hiram Ricker of Poland bought the building for $30,000. He had it taken apart, marked by section, and transported back to Maine by train. Then it was re-erected on the grounds of the Poland Spring Resort. A third floor was added, and some other alterations were made.

Today the Maine State Building is a museum with a variety of exhibits. One room contains pictures of weddings in the All Souls Chapel going back to the 1940s; another is dedicated to the Columbian Exposition. Still another room has memorabilia from the Poland Spring House, the grand hotel that mysteriously burned in 1975. The menus are particularly entertaining. In a room dedicated to Poland Spring Water, letters are displayed attesting to cures after drinking the water, along with various bottles issued over the years. Then there is a display of various advertisements used to promote the Poland Spring Resort. The resort was heavily publicized as a winter destination, complete with a toboggan slide and skating ponds.

In addition to those displays, the museum also houses the Maine Golf

Hall of Fame with many photos and golfing artifacts, including George H.W. Bush's golf bag.

There is a $3.00 charge to enter the museum, which is open from Memorial Day Weekend to Columbus Day, but closed on Sundays and Mondays. Be sure to allow plenty of time, because the museum is lots of fun to tour.

We're not through yet, as there is still more to see. Keep driving under the arch that says "Preservation Park." In the early 1900s, this Spanish-style building with a tower was built to house the water-bottling business. It is now the Poland Spring Museum and Environmental Education Center. This museum features exhibits on the history of the bottling operation. There is a very enlightening display of how water travels through the sub-strata of the earth to become Poland Spring Water. Photos lining the balcony illustrate the many famous people who visited the resort in its glory days: President Taft, President Teddy Roosevelt, Babe Ruth, Mae West, and Judy Garland are just a few. Don't bypass this building; it is very informative.

The smaller building to the rear, known as "the source," is the site of the original spring. The interior is elegant in white marble. Be sure to check this out. Both the source and the museum building are free to tour.

The park has five miles of beautifully manicured walking trails where you can breathe the fresh air and savor the views.

The next time you reach for a bottle of Poland Spring water, remember

that there is a lot more to Poland Spring than just the water. Make a note to visit and see for yourself.

As for the meal, we discovered a new restaurant to put on our favorites list—Cyndi's Dockside, located on Route 26 about a mile north of the Poland Spring Resort. It sits on the shore of Middle Range Pond with outside tables, perfect for the summer season. Open year round, the restaurant has a pine-paneled dining room with a fireplace for winter and fall visits. There were four in our party; we each ordered something different and were all completely satisfied with our choices. The menu offers plenty of seafood in addition to steak, chicken, and barbecue. At some times of the year it can be closed Mondays and Tuesdays. Call 207-998-5008 to be sure they are open before you head out. Cyndi's was the perfect ending to our day of exploration at the Poland Spring Resort.

The Ships of Liberty

Set in the midst of a pine grove on the shores of scenic Casco Bay is a memorial to the Liberty Ships built on this site during World War II.

Facing out to sea is a full-size steel mockup of the bow of a ship. There were 266 of these ships built between 1941 and 1945 at this 140-acre shipyard. Approximately 30,000 men and women worked here on as many as thirteen ships at one time. The Liberty Ships were cargo vessels carrying crucial supplies to the European Allies; without these supplies the Allies could not have won the War.

Inside the mockup is a plaque with the names of the 266 ships built here. That number, 266 ships, is just a number, but the long plaque engraved with the names of those ships helps us to convert that number to something real.

There are also three double-sided informational boards with engrossing facts, figures, and reproductions. My father was one of the 30,000 who

worked here. When I look at the informational boards, I remember stories he told me about his job. The pictures and reproductions of newspapers bring this era to life and help us to have a greater appreciation of those years. It is so important for us to have memorials like this one so we don't forget crucial episodes in our history.

Prior to the war, this area was known as Cushing's Point, a tranquil fishing community in South Portland. The land was appropriated and the natural harbor was filled in to make enough land for the shipyard to operate. At the entrance to the park, there is a polished black marble marker dedicated to the Cushing Island community.

The home of the Liberty Ship Memorial on the site of the shipyard is now known as Bug Light Park. The views of Casco Bay from the park are stunning. This gorgeous park is one jewel in the necklace of public parks that range from the Eastern Promenade in Portland to Bug Light Park and Spring Point in South Portland to Fort Williams and Two Lights in Cape Elizabeth.

Even though there are large patches of white on the landscape, the turquoise beauty of Casco Bay is still dazzling on these cold, winter days. When you visit, leave enough time to stroll along the shoreline and enjoy the beauty of this area.

The Saltwater Grille at 231 Front Street, South Portland, is about a mile away. The Grille is a full-service restaurant on the waterfront, with an outside deck for summer dining. At night the lights of Portland on the other side sparkle across the bay. Their lobster corn bisque is a favorite of mine. Include a visit to this restaurant after you view the memorial.

To reach the Liberty Ship Memorial, drive to the end of Broadway in South Portland and turn left on Breakwater Drive. Then turn right onto Madison Street, which curves to the left. Turn right off Madison Street before the entrance to the boat launch. The Cushing's Point marker is located here, and the memorial is straight ahead.

To reach the restaurant, backtrack to Broadway and turn right at the blinking light onto Sawyer Street. At the end of Sawyer Street, turn left on Front Street. The Saltwater Grille is just a few feet ahead on the right.

Cross Over the Bridge

Where Route 1 winds close to the Androscoggin River in Brunswick, there is a pedestrian bridge that crosses over to the Topsham side of the river—the Androscoggin Swinging Bridge. It's free, it's open to all, and it's fun!

This bridge was built in 1892 by John A. Roebling's Sons Company, the same company that built the Brooklyn Bridge. It was originally constructed with wooden towers, but they were replaced with steel in the early 1900s. In 2006 the bridge was renovated to its present condition. The wooden deck of the bridge is approximately 560 feet across, and the towers are approximately 332 feet high.

The bridge was built so that workers could cross the river from their homes in Topsham to the stores and mills where they worked in Brunswick.

On either side are small parks with brick-paved approaches and commemorative plaques. As you cross the bridge, you enjoy picturesque views of the river. On the Topsham side, trails and rocky outcroppings are particularly photogenic in summer or right after a snowfall. The views of the Androscoggin from the bridge are unparalleled. There are plans to connect the Topsham approach to the bridge with a riverside walkway.

There is actually very little "swing" if you walk normally across on a not-too-windy day. If you want to experience crossing in Indiana Jones style, you could move so that it would have some swing. So add some adventure to this boring winter, pretend you are Indiana Jones, and head out for the Swinging Bridge.

The bridge has been declared a Maine Historic Civil Engineering Landmark and has been added to the National Register of Historic Places.

After your adventure, head to The Great Impasta at 42 Maine Street in Brunswick. Note that the interior of this restaurant is cleverly designed to appear much larger than it is. Everything we have eaten here is delicious, and the Italian dishes are superb. I'm especially fond of their dessert brownie, which makes the perfect ending for any meal.

Remember Those Who Served

Snow, snow everywhere, with nary a sprig of green to be found. What to do? We were feeling buried in a snow cave and wanted some diversion. On a recent afternoon we decided to visit the Maine Military Museum at 50 Peary Terrace in South Portland, off Broadway near Cash Corner. This small gem is tucked onto a small plot of land in a residential area of the city.

In approximately 6,000 square feet of space are uniforms, weapons, photos, and much more. These artifacts belong to Lee Humiston, curator and director, who is a retired Air Force veteran. Private museums can be tedious, full of dusty heirlooms. But Mr. Humiston knows every single item in the museum and can relate its history. That is where this museum really shines. He will tell you about the person each uniform belonged to and how and why it reached his care. And care he does. Every artifact is clean,

polished, and carefully displayed. The stories make these artifacts come alive and speak to you.

There is the WWI uniform with mortar holes; Lee will tell you of the recovery of that Maine soldier. There is the canon ball from the bombardment of Portland (then known as Falmouth) during the Revolutionary War; that cannonball was found in the timbers of a house undergoing renovation. There are the photos of a woman and children that were found in the uniform of an unknown Union soldier; they were publicized and within six months, the soldier was identified as one from Maine.

There is the metal plaque, Number 44 of 1000, made from metal salvaged from the battleship *Maine,* sunk in the Spanish-American War.

Perhaps the most poignant and haunting display is the exact—in size and every other aspect—replica of a prisoner-of-war cell from the Vietnam War. Twenty former POWs have been here and seen the cell. Mr. Humiston will tell you their stories and how they reacted. Those stories are sober and heart-rending.

As you enter the museum, there are over 450 metal plates fastened around the perimeter of the attached banquet hall. These commemorative plates are engraved with the names of military personnel from the Spanish American War to the present. It costs $50.00 to have one added; visitors to the museum frequently purchase one for a current or deceased family member of the military. Lee himself is descended from generations of military members, each of whom has a plaque.

Mr. Humiston proudly explains that every item in the museum is authentic, with the exception of two Revolutionary War uniforms. Could there be a more gratifying way to spend a frigid winter afternoon than a visit to this unique museum? There is no charge, but donations are welcome. During the winter months, the museum is officially open on Saturdays and Sundays, but Mr. Humiston will meet you there at other times by appointment.

After touring the museum, we were ready to eat. We drove out to Broadway, turned right, and drove about one-half mile to Dock's Seafood, located at 15 Evans Street. This is one of our favorite seafood restaurants and open year-round. They serve lobsters, fried clams, shrimp and scallops, chowders, lobster rolls and non-seafood items, too. In warmer months there is outside seating. You can't go wrong by choosing Dock's.

The Wild Roses of June

June is the month when wild roses bloom along roadways and country lanes, and their sweet fragrance wafts through the air. Their robust pink color bursts forth as the longest days of the year arrive. Wild roses seem to thrive near the seashore. A trip to any beach is sure to include clusters of the fragrant blossoms.

The wild roses that proliferate here are known as *Rosa rugosa* or beach roses. After the blossoms pass, the fruit, known as rose hips, begin to develop. In late summer after they ripen, the bright red hips can be used in teas, jams, jellies, soaps, and other applications.

On a recent day we drove to Hills Beach in Biddeford and found the most extensive display of wild roses I have ever seen. It was a pure delight to drive along a road bordered by both rose and white wild roses.

Stands of roses in the foreground of a brilliant blue ocean created spectacular seascapes. What a beautiful reward for enduring the weeks of cold and dirty black snowbanks of the previous winter.

We are truly blessed to live near so much beauty that can be enjoyed free of charge. Now is the time to make at least one excursion to see the wild roses of June.

Our drive took us through Biddeford to Route 9, which we followed until the left turn toward the University of New England. An interesting sidelight of the trip is to see how this small college has emerged as a thriving university campus. As a bonus, in addition to the wild roses, there are many houses along this road that have beautiful flower gardens. Continue traveling down the Hills Beach Road to the end and enjoy the wild roses of June along the way.

If the sea air whets your appetite, Buffleheads Restaurant is located on the right side of the road as you travel toward the sea. This charming little restaurant serves lunch from 11:30 to 2:00 p.m. and reopens at 5:00 p.m. for dinner. A visit to Buffleheads is a must visit for us at least once every summer.

A Saltwater Farm in Freeport

Saltwater farms have always held a special place in American lore. The romantic ideal of a farm by the sea was the ultimate pastoral dream for bucolic life. A saltwater farm was the best of both worlds: a home that overlooks the blue ocean where you could farm the land in the golden sunshine.

The Pettengill Farm in Freeport is an authentic saltwater farm that has been preserved by the Freeport Historical Society. The saltbox-style house, built around 1810, sits on 140 acres that overlook an estuary of the Harraseeket River. In the midst of a wildflower carpet, the house is situated on a slope that sweeps down to the water. As you walk around the farmhouse, you can feel an aura of serenity in this space that is devoid of wires and all the disfiguring encroachments of modern society. Time seems to stand still here as you listen to the calls of birds and the chirping of crickets.

Mildred Pettengill and her brother Frank lived and worked the farm until Frank's death in 1960. Mildred remained there alone until 1970. The farm was acquired by the Freeport Historical Society and has been listed in the National Register of Historical Places since 1973. Once a year, in October, the farmhouse is opened to the public. A tour of the house, which lacks electricity, plumbing, and central heating, illustrates how hard life was for older generations. There are remarkable etchings, called sgraffitti, of sailing

ships dating from the War of 1812 on some of the second-story walls.

When we first started visiting the farm about twenty years ago, there were several outbuildings in a dilapidated condition which have since been razed. The Historical Society has an ongoing restoration project to return the farm to its former state. A small milk shed was renovated as an Eagle Scout project, and the barn was rebuilt just last year.

A small apple orchard on one side of the property should be a gorgeous sight when the trees are in bloom. The surrounding fields were farmed with corn, millet, oats, beans, and other vegetables. The Pettengills kept pigs, horses, cows, and oxen on the farm and harvested marsh hay and clams from the cove.

In the backyard is a flower garden that was cultivated by Mildred. She lovingly tended the garden and used discarded bricks to make paths that encircled the flowers and are still visible today.

A half-mile gravel road leads from the parking area on Pettengill Road through a splendid woodland to the farm. It takes about twelve minutes to walk in. This walk is part of the mystique of visiting the farm. You pass stands of hemlock, pine, birch, and oak trees (see how many you can identify). Listen to the calls of several species of birds and the staccato tapping of woodpeckers. Check the banks along the road for wildflowers. Look at the dappling patterns of sunlight streaming through the tree branches. Scenic stone bluffs rise from the side of the lane. Whenever I walk the road, I wonder whether Mildred and Frank had a car or if they traveled by horse and cart.

This farm is a wonderful resource and example of a lifestyle gone by. It is well worth a visit for the beauty and to ponder life on a saltwater farm.

From the center of Freeport, take Bow Street for 1.2 mile to Pettengill Road on the right. There is a small parking area there and an informational sign at the beginning of the gravel road.

After your walking visit to the Farm, you will probably be ready for a meal. We suggest the Muddy Rudder on Route 1 in Yarmouth just beyond the Freeport line. The beige-shingled building, on the Cousins River, is classic New England style, and the interior, with its soothing greens and windows on the water, has a welcoming and relaxing ambience. They serve lunch and dinner, offering seafood, meat, and vegetarian entries, with daily specials.

Tarry a While by the Pineland Pond

Spring at last! After being held hostage by snow and cold during the grueling winter, we craved warm sunshine. So on a recent 60-degree day, we headed out to Pineland Farm in New Gloucester for a much needed respite.

We took Route 115 from Yarmouth and continued up Route 231 to New Gloucester. Although the trees were still leafless, the sky was a spectacular cloudless blue, and the wind was dormant—just a gorgeous day to be outside.

The approach to Pineland Farm is impressive. Rounding a corner, the road crests on a hill and then declines amid fields crisscrossed by white fences. A large red barn stands on the right, and Pineland's Equine Center is on the left. We continued straight on 231, past the main Pineland Campus to the Pond at Pineland on the left, where we parked in a small parking lot.

The pond is small and sits at the end of the campus lawns next to the forest. There are log benches on one side and stone benches on the other. What a beautiful setting to enjoy the birdsong, the warmth of the sun, and the fragrance of the spring air! The ice was gone from the pond, and minnows darted about.

A scenic gazebo basked in the sun on the lawn beyond the pond, while a rustic bridge led from the area of the pond to the campus. A patch of daffodils was just coming into bloom beside the pond.

A picnic table next to the pond invited us to sit and dine. The Welcome Center at Pineland offers sandwiches, soups, salads, and baked goodies. We made a visit there, chose a lunch to go, and returned to the picnic table to dine in nature's ambience.

The Welcome Center also sells fresh produce; Pineland cheeses and meats; and Maine-made crafts, books, and toys. There is a large, interactive display board of the entire Pineland Campus. A visit here is a pleasant way to shop and spend an afternoon.

A few hours in the serene setting of the Pineland Pond was a splendid way to welcome spring. In late spring and summer, there is a beautiful garden across the road from the pond, which we will return to enjoy in a couple of months.

Christmas at the Monastery

Every Christmas I like to find some new event or place to visit to keep the holiday special and a little bit new. This year on a cold, blustery Sunday, we visited St. Anthony's Franciscan Monastery in Kennebunkport. The estate of William Campbell was purchased in 1947 by exiled Lithuanian Franciscans and converted to a monastery. The park-like grounds, which sweep down to the Kennebunk River, are very handsome and invite meditative walks.

In front of Our Lady of Lourdes Shrine, set in a wooded grove, the monastery has displayed a very striking, life-size nativity scene. The nativity, in its tranquil setting in front of the impressive grotto-like shrine, is captivating.

As you enter the grounds, a sculpture, known as "The Triad" stands on the left. It was sculpted by a Lithuanian, Vytautas K. Jonynas, for the Vatican Pavilion at the 1964-65 World's Fair in New York. St. Anthony's Chapel, built in 1965-66, has magnificent interior decorations also designed by Mr. Jonynas.

There are several other religious structures on the grounds, all Lithuanian in style. This whole complex is very interesting, but because of the frigid wind, we didn't explore as much as I would have liked.

The Tudor-style main building is now a guest house used by visitors to Kennebunkport. The restaurant is open to the public for breakfast on Saturdays and Sundays from 7:30 to 9:00. A gift shop on the lower level of the church sells a wide variety of religious items and books.

A visit to St. Anthony's Monastery, located at 26 Beach Avenue, Kennebunk Beach, can provide a serene interval in the hectic Holiday season. St Anthony's Monastery is located at 26 Beach Avenue, Kennebunk Beach, Maine.

After our visit to the monastery on such a frigid day, we were ready for a bowl of hot chowder. We returned to Route 9, proceeded about four and one-half miles to Route One, and turned left to the Maine Diner. Their seafood chowder was the perfect choice for this wintry day. For dessert we chose a slice of their reasonably priced and delicious pie. When you visit the Maine Diner, don't forget to visit their well-stocked gift shop.

Stonehenge in America?

Before there were paper calendars and before there were computers, people kept track of the months and seasons by astrological means. The ancient peoples noted that the sun and moon were always in predictable locations at the same time every year. Most civilizations built structures to keep track of the movement of the sun and moon. Everyone has heard of Stonehenge in England, but did you know that right across the border in New Hampshire there is a megalithic stone site?

Located in Salem, New Hampshire, the site, estimated to be at least 4,000 years old, is known as America's Stonehenge. Carbon dating done in several places confirms walls as old as 2000 BCE. This site has also been used by Native Americans and in the 1700 and 1800s by a family named Pattee. There are many stone caves, huts, and walls, and Mr. Pattee apparently used some of the huts for storage.

Some of the chambers and walls appear to have been constructed on a particular astrological axis, both east–west and north–south. Markings on some stones are similar to those found in ancient sites in Europe. One particular hole is similar to those found on Malta. When this site was rediscovered in the 1930s, speculation was that it had been built by Irish Culdee monks. Unfortunately, there was some disturbance of the original site by the main excavator at that time, so there seems to be no definite conclusion as to who actually built the structures on the site.

As I walked around the huts and walls, I marveled, as I always do, that I was walking where people had lived and walked thousands of years ago. To me, that is awesome! Whoever occupied the site over the years, it does not detract from the ancient dating and the alignment of the stones. There are even petroglyphs in some of the huts. Again, while they have been studied by experts, there is no consensus on who made them.

There is a sacrificial table with a channel, possibly a drain, carved along the top. This slab is near the "oracle speaking tube" and chamber, a stone-lined tube through which sounds travel. Someone in the chamber above could speak into the tube, and the words would appear to come from under the sacrificial slab—hence an "oracle" could be speaking.

This whole site is absolutely fascinating, as there are few truly ancient structures in North America. The astronomical arrangement of monolithic stones was proven in 1979 to be accurate for both spring and fall equinox sunsets.

It takes about 15 minutes to follow the astronomical trail to view the True North Stone, the Summer Solstice Sunrise Stone, the May Day Monolith, the November First Stone, and several other markers. The ancient peoples were experts on viewing and interpreting astrological patterns. America's Stonehenge is open year round, except Thanksgiving and Christmas. In the winter they offer snowshoeing around the woodland site. (As a sidelight, there is a small herd of alpacas here to entertain you with their perpetual smiles!) For an interesting and entertaining excursion, you won't regret a trip to these rocky remnants from prehistory.

Directions (from their brochure): From I-93: Take Exit 3 and follow Route 111 east for 4.5 miles. Watch for our sign just past North Salem Village Shops. Turn right at the intersection with the traffic light. Follow this road for 1 mile. Entrance is on the right. From 495: Take Exit 50 to Route 97 North towards Salem. Follow approximately 4 miles. At your first set of lights (97 Shoppes will be on your right), turn right and follow approximately 4 miles. America's Stonehenge will be on your left.

After this walking and viewing, we're hungry—so on to Warren's Lobster House in Kittery. Warren's is one of our favorite restaurants—perhaps our most favorite. They have an extensive salad bar with to-die-for pumpkin bread. This salad bar accompanies meals, or you can have it alone or with my preference, grilled shrimp. Scrumptious desserts are served in smaller portions (fewer calories) so everyone can enjoy one. No trip to the New Hampshire border is complete without a stop at Warren's.

In the Heart of Harpswell

Up hill and down dale, by meadows and stands of forests, Route 123 meanders down the Harpswell peninsula. Leave Brunswick on Route 123, the Harpswell Neck Road, and almost immediately you are in a rural area. There are no fast food drive-ins or strip malls; this is the way life used to be. The Harpswell peninsula is very narrow, and occasionally it is possible to catch glimpses of the ocean inlets on either side.

This is a very pretty drive. On the left side out of Brunswick are two ponds filled with rose-colored lilies. Several horses frequently graze in a meadow, also on the left side of the road. On the right side, a large, white barn sits atop a hill overlooking an apple orchard, a gorgeous sight when in bloom. Old farms abound on both sides of the roadway.

About ten miles down Route 123 is a cluster of historical buildings that I call the heart of Harpswell. Situated very close to a curve in the road,

Harpswell's Old Meeting House is on the right. Built between 1757 and 1759, the meeting house has some interesting features. The pulpit rises ten feet from the floor to the same level as the gallery. Was this so the preacher could be better heard by those seated in the gallery, or so that he could better watch over those in attendance? One floorboard in the deacon's box is said to be 29-1/2 inches wide. At the time the meetinghouse was built, there was a law that trees measuring more than 24 inches in diameter were reserved for masts for the king's Navy. It's interesting to speculate on the reason for flouting this royal decree!

In 1968 the Harpswell Meeting House was designated as a national historic landmark. Today the Old Meeting House serves as the town office and polling place. During the summer months, it is open to the public. The old burying ground behind the meeting house contains the graves of early settlers. The granite posts in front of the cemetery served as hitching posts to secure horses.

Across the street is the Elijah Kellogg Church Congregational, built in 1843. This church is a prime example of the many white Congregational churches found throughout New England. It has been well maintained over the years and is currently undergoing renovations.

To the left of the church, set back from the roadway perhaps 100 feet, is the Harpswell Cattle Pound, erected in 1793. Pounds were necessary in colonial times to corral stray cattle and to keep them from trampling and destroying settlers' crops.

Across the street are the Harpswell Centennial Hall and the Harpswell Historic Park. The hall, built in 1829, was used as a school until 1913. A beautiful garden and park are in the forefront of the hall. The colorful garden and walking paths are a peaceful spot for quiet contemplation.

These few buildings provided the necessary support for a New England community to thrive. A drive here seems like time travel. As I walk around the buildings in this area, time seems to stand still. We are indeed fortunate to have communities like this preserved so that we can appreciate our heritage.

Continue down Route 123 and enjoy the lovely old farmhouses and views of the ocean on both sides of the peninsula. If you turn right onto the Basin Point Road, then turn right again onto the Ash Point Road and travel about a mile to the end, you will arrive at the Dolphin Marina and Restaurant. This is one of our all-time favorite seasonal restaurants. The setting, at the end of the point with views of the Atlantic all around, is superb. And the food is fabulous. They are famous (and my favorite spot) for haddock chowder and blueberry muffins.

For a memorable summertime excursion, a road trip to Harpswell and the Dolphin is unbeatable.

The Temple at Ocean Park

Known for its wide, white sand beaches, Old Orchard Beach is a popular summer vacation destination. Situated in the middle of the beach is the summer community of Ocean Park. Founded in 1881 by the Free Will Baptist organization, Ocean Park was part of the Chautauqua movement. Most Chautauqua sites were near a body of water and pine trees—the perfect description of the Ocean Park site.

Ocean Park has been described as an experience. There is a ten-week "season" every summer when participants come to share education, entertainment, religious services, and camaraderie.

The Temple is their main meeting and religious services building. Built in 1881 at a cost of $3,592, the Temple is constructed of pine and hemlock in an octagonal shape, a popular design at that time. With a seating capacity of approximately 800 people, the ceiling rises to a height of 65 feet at the cupola,

a plan that allows for a very spacious and airy feeling. The interior is unfinished, so the unique construction is visible. The slope of the roof is quite steep and ends at the cupola. This building, well over a hundred years old, is in excellent condition and has been well maintained.

There is a three-stop chest organ in the Temple; the wooden parts of the organ are cherry and mahogany. A carillon, installed in 2008, chimes at noon and 5:00 p.m.

The Bell Tower is located adjacent to the Temple. Wooden steps lead up to a deck that has benches for seating. At night the bell tower is lighted and is known as a beacon of welcome.

The Temple, Bell Tower, Porter Memorial Hall, and B.C. Jordan Memorial Hall comprise the district called "Ocean Park Historic Buildings" and have been named to the National Register of Historic Places. The Porter and Jordan buildings are used for offices and meetings. The Temple is the geographic center of the Ocean Park site, and the entire four-building space, set in a grove of pine trees, is protected by covenants.

The area surrounding and across from Temple Square has been kept open. It has often been used for meditation and is a welcome respite from the

hustle and bustle of this busy summer area. Across the street is the Temple Garden, complete with benches for quiet contemplation.

The non-denominational services and various entertainment events are all open to the public, some for a nominal fee. I have attended some very enjoyable performances at the Temple. There is a resident chorus, a brass ensemble, and a bell-ringing group. To sit in the Temple on a warm summer evening, enjoying a musical performance with the scent of balsam and the fans moving gentle breezes through the building, is a summer tradition at Ocean Park. The Temple and the Ocean Park area are well worth a summer visit.

For our meal after our visit to the Temple, we chose the Lobster Claw Pound and Restaurant at 41 Ocean Park Road, Saco. This is the place for a summer seafood feast of lobster, fried clams, and the like. The Lobster Claw is a seasonal restaurant that closes from October until Mother's Day and is open only on weekends in May, early June and September.

The Way Way Store

Remember when a shiny, copper penny would buy a piece of candy? You can still find that candy today. The Way Way Store on Route 112 in Saco carries it, but it will cost you six cents. Just step across the threshold into a general store from 90 years ago.

The candy is all there: Tootsie Rolls, Bit of Honey, Good and Plenty, Bazooka Gum, Laffy Taffy, Mary Janes, Mint Juleps, Boston Baked Beans, and many more. You can almost see children standing on tiptoe to see what scrumptious morsels of candy are waiting in glass jars for them to choose.

The store is packed with nostalgic products and memorabilia. You will see a Wheaties box with Jim Thorpe's picture, an Orange Crush sign, a Blackstone Cigars advertisement, and numerous cans and tins of products from a bygone era. There are displays of old license plates and glass milk bottles. Every wall, corner, and shelf is a history lesson from Grandfather's days.

Peter Scontras, the proprietor, was wearing a jaunty straw panama hat the day I visited. He loves to show visitors some of the treasures he has acquired over the years, including a GE Handy Hot portable washing machine and a cast iron sausage maker that converts into a fruit or cider press. He also has a coffee grinder, a weight and fortune machine, and a vintage juke box.

The building opened as a general store in 1924. The exterior still has the original handmade concrete blocks painted in red and white. Over the years, gasoline was added, and the store became a favorite stopping place. There are still two original gas pumps out front: Tydol and Flying A brands (remember those?). The counters, shelves, and cash register are the originals. There is a soda fountain where you can still purchase ice cream. Local lore has it that the name came from people referring to the store as "way, way out there."

The Way Way Store was placed on the National Register of Historic Places in 1995.

The store is open every day in the summer and Saturdays and Sundays in the fall. It is closed from January to May. For a trip down memory lane, take a ride to Saco and relive childhood memories of sweet tastes and treats.

A visit to the Way Way Store is not complete without taking advantage of their vintage soda fountain. They serve ice cream cones, sundaes, and old fashioned frappes. You can call ahead to see if your visit is going to be on one of the days that they are serving pie. After sampling the candy and having an ice cream dessert, we bypassed dinner on this trip.

The Three Gs of Paris Hill

For quite some time I have wanted to visit Paris Hill, a village that is part of South Paris. In 1973 it was named to the National Register of Historic Places. So earlier this summer, we made the trip.

After passing through the center of South Paris on Route 26, the road to Paris Hill leads to the right. You can't miss it, as there is a sign designating the way. The road rises gradually to a higher elevation. As you reach the top of the hill, you enter an area of stately homes with wide green lawns and tall shade trees. Most of the homes here were built between 1805 and 1885. Several of them have descriptive names: Crossroads, The Birches, Lyonsden.

This was an era of gracious living, when each home had a parlor used only for very special or serious occasions. My imagination takes over here, and I picture ladies in a carriage, drawn by a horse trotting smartly down the road, on their way to afternoon tea.

The classic village green is in the center of the district with streets located around its perimeter. On one corner is the impressive First Baptist Church, completed in 1838. The bell in the tower is one of the last surviving bells cast by the Paul Revere Foundry. It is said that one Fourth of July, the bell was kept continuously ringing by boys working in relays.

Hannibal Hamlin, vice president under Abraham Lincoln, was born here in Paris Hill in 1809. His birthplace is a grand white house facing the village green at the top of Paris Hill. The views of the White Mountains from this location are spectacular. A plaque in remembrance of Hannibal Hamlin is located on the village green.

Near Hamlin's birthplace is a small building housing a community library and a museum. Constructed of granite blocks, this building was the Oxford County Jail from 1822 through 1896. A plaque notes that a descendant of Hannibal Hamlin presented it to the Ladies of Paris Hill in 1901, and it has been operated as a library since that time. As you enter the library, one of the first things you see is a large sign, a throwback to the time when it was the jail: "ALL PERSONS ARE POSITIVELY FORBIDDEN TALKING WITH THE PRISONERS." The museum has some interesting exhibits that are worth viewing.

Most of the houses in the district are classic New England clapboard structures. However, a handsome brick house, built in 1926 and situated near the Common, was the office of Oxford County until 1895. Today it is privately owned and not open to the public.

After we had visited Paris Hill, I later found an online site that offers a

map for a walking route of the village. I would recommend going to this site and printing out the map: http://www.hamlin.lib.me.us/walkingtour.html. I'm planning to do just that, and to make another visit to Paris Hill. This visit, however, we walked without the map and absorbed the serenity of the area.

As you stroll around Paris Hill, you feel a sense of peacefulness and tranquility. Life in nineteenth century Paris Hill was genteel, and that gentility is still reflected there today. Skateboards and graffiti are out of place here. Visiting Paris Hill is a grand and gracious experience.

Now, where shall we eat? We are not very familiar with Oxford County restaurants, so we surfed the web for suggestions and chose the Smilin' Moose Tavern at 10 Market Square in South Paris. The décor is moose here, moose there, and moose everywhere. Can't get more mid-Maine than that. The restaurant was clean and we felt welcomed into a friendly neighborhood eatery. We ordered hamburgers and were pleased with them. This was a fun place to end our day's excursion to Paris Hill.

References

Lear, Alex. "Funds sought for 'Swinging Bridge' repairs," *The Falmouth Forecaster*, 5 July 2013, 4.

This work has also consulted sources from the following organizations:

Hamlin Memorial Library / Museum
American Society of Civil Engineers
Ocean Park Association
Lincoln County Historical Association
Poland Spring Preservation Society
U.S. National Register of Historic Places

About the Author, Lois Stailing

A Maine native, Lois earned a BA in history from the University of Maine. Her love of history and travel led her to seek out unique and beautiful places. A desire to share these places has inspired Lois to start her blog and now her book, *Nearaway Places*. A mother and grandmother, Lois is extremely proud of her son and two grandsons.